Bull

Beautiful Pictures & Interesting Facts Children Book About Bull

Renee Wood

Renee Wood

Copyright © 2018 by Renee Wood

All rights reserved. No part of this book may be used or reproduced in any manner whatsoever without the express written permission of the publisher except for the use of brief quotations in a book review

Image Credits: Royalty free images reproduced under license from various stock image repositories. Under a creative commons licenses.

I am a bull.

I am a big boy cow.

I am from the cattle family.

We have long and thick horns.

My body is very big and strong.

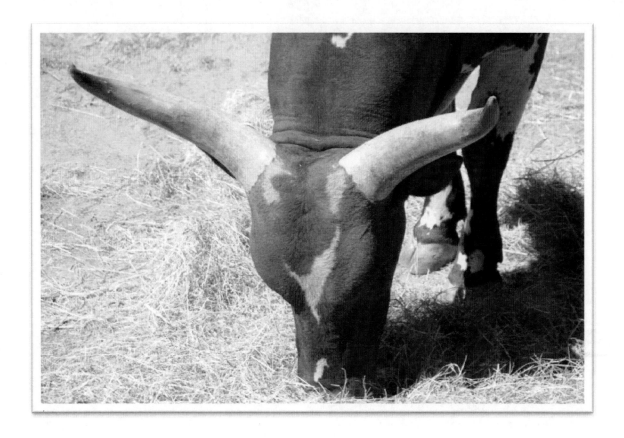

I have four strong legs that help me run.

A leader to other cows, I can be.

I can live in the wild and in farms.

While bullfighting is my game,

It is not really that fun.

The color red angers me so much.

Men in moving red capes better run.

Bulls like me love grasses, corns, and plants.

We do not like eating fish or meat.

We say "Moo... Moo..." loud and proud.

It means "Come on, get up on your feet!"

Bulls are also fathers to little baby cows.

We can have 1 baby calf or 2.

Then mommy cow feeds them with milk,

So they will grow up strong like me and you.

Yes, I am a bull – brave, horned, and proud.

I can keep everyone around me safe and sound.